THE MONOTONY MANACLE

THE MONOTONY MANACLE

THE #1

INCENTIVE KILLER AND WHAT TO DO ABOUT IT

DAVID COOLS

Copyright © 2017 David Cools
Published by David Cools

All rights reserved. No part of this publication may be reproduced, stored in a retrieval system or transmitted, in any form, or by any means, electronic, mechanical, recorded, photocopied, or otherwise, without the prior written permission of both the copyright owner and the above publisher of this book, except by a reviewer who may quote brief passages in a review.

The scanning, uploading, and distribution of this book via the Internet or via any other means without the permission of the publisher is illegal and punishable by law. Please purchase only authorized electronic editions and do not participate in or encourage electronic piracy of copyrightable materials. Your support of the author's rights is appreciated.

Designed by Vince Pannullo
Printed in the United States of America by RJ Communications.

ISBN: 978-0-578-19077-8

Contents

Chapter 1: Craftsman or Wage Slave: Must Work Be Drudgery? 9
Chapter 2: Worker Satisfaction 13
Chapter 3: Building the Part or Building the Whole 19
Chapter 4: Considering the Craftsman 23
Chapter 5: The Emotions of a Craftsman 27
Chapter 6: The Modern Factory Lacks a Beginning, Middle, and End 31
Chapter 7: The Assembly Line 39
Chapter 8: Utility and Beauty 45
Chapter 9: Rhythm 51
Chapter 10: Incentives 53
Chapter 11: Ways Incentive Is Killed in The Modern Workplace 59
Chapter 12: Solutions 73
Chapter 13: Maximize Incentive Effectiveness 85
Chapter 14: Worker Competition 91
Chapter 15: Goals and Ends Are Not the Same 95
Chapter 16: Solutions to Rework and Rhythm Problems 97
Chapter 17: A Brighter Future 101

To my Dad and the Craftsman in All of Us

Chapter One

Craftsman or Wage Slave: Must Work Be Drudgery?

FEW people are born to wealth or privilege, and, so, most have no choice but to acquire their wealth by working. Of these people, the greater number work for companies, either in leadership roles or as subordinates carrying out the directives of their leaders. There are many who operate their own businesses and a few who work alone. It is a condition of man that he must work, not just play or spend his time in study. Even those who do not need to work for economic reasons still have a psychological need to work for their own fulfillment. It is this time and effort spent in work that we will examine here.

This book is primarily directed to people who run their own businesses or to managers employed by a company. However, it could also be useful for the employees of the companies themselves, since more accountability, control, and innovation is being sought at the lower levels of companies today. The owners and managers will gain a greater understanding of what motivates some people to work harder than others, or, to put it another way, why some people are so much happier in their work environments than others. With this knowledge, people in supervisory roles can learn how to organize workplaces and formulate incentive plans that will maximize worker productivity. This will be a win for the employer, for the employee, and for the larger community. This book will also be of great interest of those who seek an alternative to the present corporate structure of our economy.

To accomplish our task, the book will focus on the Achilles' heel of the modern manufacturing plant—the emotional dissatisfaction that flows from specialization. As jobs become more specialized, and as each worker performs smaller parts of a production process, each worker becomes more proficient at whatever part he does. However, in the process, the worker becomes more stressed and less satisfied with his work life. This is not to say that the worker necessarily gets less done; in fact, he usually gets more done. But at what cost?

We can't deny the increased productivity that results from specialization. Indeed, we cannot proceed without reminding ourselves of the two main reasons for this increased productivity. The first is the specialization and division of labor that Adam Smith so aptly described in his work The Wealth of Nations. The second is the introduction of the assembly line popularly attributed to Henry Ford and the production of his automobile. However, I will argue that a great deal more productivity would be realized from these practices if we recovered the best of the economic practices of pre-industrial society. By revisiting the world of the craftsmen of old, we will be able to discover why most modern efforts to remedy job dissatisfaction have failed and why happiness on the job remains so elusive. I am not going to try to address all of the requirements for a happy or contented life, of course, but only to address those things that inspire, motivate, and bring satisfaction to one's work. I believe that you will enjoy this discovery as much as I have. You will discover how much you have in common with the craftsman of old. And you will find that, the more your experience on the job resembles his, the happier—and the more productive—you (and your employees) will be!

Chapter Two

Worker Satisfaction

At times we miss the most important aspects of our experience, because they are so obvious that we tune them out. This usually happens when we think about work. We all work. Everyone talks about it. Most people don't like work, but some do. Either way, most of us have become so accustomed to work that familiarity blinds us to the elements that bring joy to our work. Advertisers know this numbing effect of familiarity and constantly vary their marketing tactics. When a business first puts up a billboard on a major highway, everyone looks at it. It's new and different so it grabs the attention. But eventually motorists tune it out as it becomes more familiar. So the business adds a blinking light or some such gadget to the billboard. Again, it will grab the public's attention for a while, but then it too is tuned out. Maybe a picture of an attractive woman is used next; and so the process goes on. All this to try to keep attention on something that has become familiar and so passes unnoticed.

So what are the keys to abiding job satisfaction that may have passed unnoticed?

There are three of them:

- The worker enjoys the job itself
- The worker has a sense of accomplishment or completeness in his work
- The worker is recognized by others for his accomplishment

--The first of the keys seems fairly obvious. If a dental hygienist doesn't like working in people's mouths, there's not a lot that can be done to make her job enjoyable. Or if a person really likes books and teaching and finds himself framing houses, he probably won't be happy in his work. He must find a job that suits his disposition, if possible. So the first point may be divided into two concerns: whether the craft the worker is doing is suited to his disposition, and whether the work environment allows for joy in his job.

Regarding the first concern, how a person ends up with a particular job and whether it suits his disposition is not my focus here. I won't be concerned with job placement. But I will be very concerned about the suitability of the work environment, and we will see that optimizing the work place can maximize the happiness of all workers, even those who may be unsuited for a particular job. You will see how this plays out when we compare medieval craftsmen with contemporary workers.

Regarding our second key, - a sense of achievement

and fulfillment in one's work again seems fairly obvious. Just think how displeasing it is to be interrupted at work; how frustrated we get when close to completing a project and an obstacle is thrown in our way; how many times we feel a sense of futility about a job that we are required to do because it seems not to serve any useful purpose.

Isn't the boredom of drudgery a common thread that runs through the complaints of employees, across a very broad spectrum of professions? And isn't it true that the more a man has this feeling of drudgery, the more he feels like a slave? We hear people use this terminology when they refer to themselves as "corporate slaves." What should interest us here is that drudgery and slavery are connected in employees' minds.

There is a commonality between these two concepts—namely, a kind of constant repetition in one's activity and a loss of control. The worker is slave to a procedure or a boss that limits his activity to a rote action. Imagine the stone suppliers in the quarries that supplied the marble for Rome's beautiful buildings. Each worker conveyed stones from one area to another, day after day, year after year. These tasks were generally done by slaves, as free men were left to do more complicated tasks involving more sophisticated work such as sculpting, saddle making, shoe making, furniture building, and the like. Typically the craftsman would make a complete product, whereas the slave was left to do repetitive tasks that had no apparent end.

We can see this same phenomenon in the cotton fields of the antebellum South where the harvesting of cotton and other mundane tasks were largely done by slaves. When one's work becomes repetitive and controlled, it becomes drudgery. Hence, it becomes slavish. Worker satisfaction increases as these experiences of boredom and monotony decrease. A glimpse of the way out of this trap can be seen if we consider a shoemaker in a medieval village.

Imagine, if you will, a small girl being taken to a medieval shoemaker to be fitted for a new pair of shoes. After having measured his little friend for the right size, the shoemaker constructs a shoe for her—the whole shoe, from beginning to end. Having made the whole shoe, he has the satisfaction of putting it on the little girl himself, to the delight of all present. Indeed, this observation will lead us to more extensive considerations of the nature of work in the following chapters. But first we must understand negative attitudes toward work if we are to find a way to change them into more positive experiences like those of our shoemaker.

Let's turn our attention to you for a moment, and gauge your level of satisfaction in your work: Do you build a complete product from beginning to end? Or, do you build only a part of a final product and others build the rest?

It is virtually certain that those of you who build a complete product enjoy your work much more than those who produce only a part of a finished product. The study of the medieval craftsman will help us to understand why this is so and to find solutions to the widespread problem of drudgery in the work place. For those who wish to pursue their fortunes outside the modern corporate structure, our study of the craftsman will be of particular interest. The study of the medieval craftsman will also shed light on the third element of job satisfaction—recognition of one's achievement.

Everyone appreciates recognition of good work. Who is there that doesn't like kudos, pats on the back, affirmation of a job well done? When these recognitions are properly aligned with other aspects of an employee's sense of fulfillment, they make a lasting impression. They then become a powerful inducement to work harder, accomplish more and achieve even greater satisfaction. We will see that whatever form recognition takes, if it is separated from this sense of fulfillment, it loses its effectiveness.

Usually when a person likes what he does, he doesn't consider his activity a job, so much as an art or a craft. Why is this? To discover what inclines a person to like or dislike his work is the key to better understanding the worker and, consequently, to fashioning a more congenial and productive workplace.

Chapter Three

Building the Part or Building the Whole

ALL work is the doing and activity that provides results or brings into existence some product. There are two ways in which a person can make a final product:

- He builds the whole thing himself (the medieval craftsman)
- He builds part of the object, and others build the remainder (the specialist of today)

By contrasting these two types of workers, we discover the vast differences between their experience (i.e., why the craftsman derived so much satisfaction from his work while the specialist of today sorely lacks it). To see this contrast between the medieval craftsman and the modern specialist is to grasp the central thesis of this book.

To do this, we will use the term "craftsman" to denote the worker who fashions a complete product from beginning to end. An example of such a craftsman is the pre–Industrial Revolution shoemaker, who would craft a whole shoe from beginning to end. Another example from this era is the blacksmith, who would forge a whole rifle from beginning to end. These craftsmen worked on every piece of a whole product and then assembled the pieces. Today, most workers in the assembly field only craft a small part of each final product. The shoemaker of today would likely stand at a molding machine that spits out thousands of soles per day. He would never touch the whole, finished shoe. The worker may never see a complete product unless he were to visit another part of the factory or another factory altogether. The specialist of today is one who, though he may be very good at what he does, only does one small, uncomplicated task over and over.

The medieval firearm manufacturer (a blacksmith) would forge every part of the whole rifle separately and then assemble it once he had completed all the parts. He might forge the barrel first and then the breech. He would next punch the holes for the stock attachments, and then he would forge the trigger, the hammer, and the finger guard, and so on. He would then lay all his pieces out in order and start assembling the firearm. After all this activity, there would be a finished firearm.

Two observations are important here. First, every firearm the blacksmith would make would be a little different from all the others, as much as he may have tried to make each identical. Rarely could a trigger or hammer be substituted for another without some kind of reworking. Second, there would be a lot of time spent between setting up his tools and the creation of each different part.

A cursory look at the modern factory will reveal that today's manufacturing methods and processes seek to eliminate both of these problems. Modern manufacturers seek to make exact copies of each part so that any given part in a product would be interchangeable with that part in another identical finished product. For example, a broken hammer on a firearm could be replaced with a new one, identical to the first. If a hammer is switched from one firearm to another of the same type, the piece would function exactly the way it did on the original. Additionally, these manufacturers seek to reduce the amount of time spent on producing each part of the final product and to lessen the time involved with setup and preparation for making each part. Hence, at present, we design workplaces in which, usually, each worker makes an individual part.

As factories grew, they were set up such that one man or group of men fashioned a trigger, another a trigger guard, and yet another a hammer, and so on. This allowed each person to become more proficient at his task because he had less variation to deal with. His concentration could be focused fully on that one part, and the repetitiveness of his task would enable him to make almost identical pieces. The setup time was drastically reduced, as his tools remained the same and his workstation never varied.

Something else became clear to those who studied these processes. The more focused and specialized the workstation became, the more the operation lent itself to being done by a machine. For example, a man whose job it was to place a screw in a pre-drilled hole could be replaced by a conveyor belt and a machine that could turn a screw. Hence, the manufacturing of the product became less a human-operated, manual activity and more a machine-operated, automated activity. In consequence, the production of exact copies became easy, deviations could be reduced, and a tremendous increase in productivity ensued. The less a worker did in building the final product, the more specialized his operation became, and the amount of identical parts a factory could produce increased.

Throughout the Industrial Revolution, it was widely assumed that producing more products, faster, and with greater precision, was a good thing. But little attention was given to the effect of this kind of production on the human beings who produced and consumed the products. The appearance of factory production usually meant the disappearance of the craftsman from the economic landscape.

Chapter Four

Considering the Craftsman

EVERY person is a craftsman at heart. Everyone, sooner or later, finds himself performing a determinate set of activities to bring about some intended product.

It will be helpful at this point in our discussion to delve into the causes at play in the craftsman's making of a product, and then consider the emotions that he experiences when fashioning his product.

Following these investigations, we will compare the medieval craftsman with the assembly line worker of today, and see how the emotions of these two are similar and how their emotions differ.

We will then be in a position to examine how the modern worker's setup could be made to mimic that of the medieval craftsman and so be more suited to his nature, and finally we can undertake a consideration of how new incentives, when designed to enrich the emotional experience of the craftsman through each phase of his work, will be more effective than conventional incentives.

A firm grasp of these potential changes in the modern workplace will empower managers and workers to achieve increased productivity. More importantly, the application of this knowledge will create much more satisfied, more motivated, and happier workers.

Beginning then with the causes involved in the craftsman's making of a product, we must first say that every art is ordered to the making of something. The sculptor makes statues. The painter makes paintings. And the same could be said of the writer who crafts an article or a book. In the menial arts, the same holds true. Saddle makers make saddles. Carpenters make tables. Machinists make tools.

The most effective way to explain the activity of a craftsman when he works is to start with the philosophical principle, what is first in intention is last in execution. This statement lends itself nicely to the task of dissecting the concept of work.

Aristotle, in his work The Physics, observes four causes that go into the making of some object—four things that, when joined together, result in the final object. First, there is the intention of the artist to make something—some vision of his, some picture in his mind of what he would like to exist. Thus, the carpenter, for example, has a picture in his mind of the chair that he wants to fashion. Even before he has tools, material, or anything else, he has an end in mind, a product that he intends to bring into existence. This is what Aristotle calls the final cause of the object's being. Secondly, there is the material that will be used to build the object. For his chair, the carpenter collects wood. This is the material cause. Thirdly, there is the form that the wood must take on in order for it to become the chair. This is called the formal cause—the form it has that distinguishes it from a cup, for example, or a statue of Venus. Fourthly, there is the efficient cause, or what is sometimes called the agent cause. This is the craftsman actually carrying out the necessary steps to produce the object of art. So, in the case of the carpenter, when he is actually drilling, sawing, filing, and nailing, he is performing the role of the agent in producing the effect. In this case, the effect is the chair.

Imagine the carpenter as he builds a chair, and note the four causes at work as they perform their separate roles in the chair's coming to be. When the carpenter decides to build a chair, he draws the chair he wishes to build. This picture, whether drawn on paper or simply existing in his mind, is the final cause. It is the end to which he directs his activity. This end is what motivates him to act. This is the thing that he wishes to bring into reality through his activity. Then he must shape the wood in such a manner as to constitute a chair. This would differ, say, from the shape of the wood assembled in such a manner as to constitute a table So, we see there is a form of chairness, as opposed to a form of tableness, that determines how the assembled wood is finally shaped. The carpenter must form the artifact to this shape. This shape is the formal cause of the chair. We can see that two of the causes of the chair, the formal cause and final cause, are the same in description with respect to the kind of thing made. They are nonetheless distinguished as separate causes when they are related to the act of making.

Even though he may intend to build a chair, the carpenter will get nowhere without the material necessary to build it; at a minimum, he must have wood. Usually another man, such as a miller, would provide him with lumber. So the carpenter now has the material to build the chair. This is the material cause of the chair.

Last but not least, the carpenter must do something. The carpenter, well-intentioned as he may be, must become an agent. The sawing, the pounding, the drilling, the carving—all this to bring the chair into existence out of a pile of wood. The carpenter himself is the agent cause. He is the agent that does the work. He is the artist.

Chapter Five

The Emotions of a Craftsman

LET'S now follow a craftsman's emotions as he goes through his characteristic activity of making something; we'll consider his emotions at the beginning, middle, and end of his making.

First, before he begins, there is an excitement at the prospect of completing a project, something that will be the fruit of his work. Many hobbyists experience this when they lie awake at night figuring out every detail of what they want to build. Engineers, research and development scientists, and the like experience this when they anticipate completing their projects. As the image of the desired object becomes more complete in the artist's mind, there grows in him an urge to actually begin work on the project. At this point, there exists the anticipated joy of the object's completion and also the desire to begin. If all things are in order to start the project, he will pick up his tools and begin.

When first beginning his task, there will be an urgency to his acts. The final end will be too far off to be immediately anticipated, yet the artist will still be fresh. He will be rested and full of energy as he progresses through the initial stages of his work. As time goes on, however, he will begin to tire. He will begin to reflect on the amount of work he has completed, and rather than comparing it directly to the end result, he will usually begin to anticipate when he will be halfway through his task. This is because he will have at least some satisfaction in having accomplished a definable amount of work at the halfway point. If conditions permit, he will take a break and replenish his body. He will also take the opportunity to reinvigorate his mind and soul.

It is at this point that he will contemplate the object he has partially shaped. He will take some joy in the work he has accomplished, and he will begin anew, anticipating completion of the object. Often this is when he will compare the work done thus far with the original plan he had of the finished project. This might take the form of pulling out his written plan. However, he might just as easily compare the partially completed project with the picture in his mind. A renewed and refreshed desire will begin to well up inside of him, and, with a face of determination, he will again pick up his tools and get to work.

This time, there will be a sense that he is on the downhill side of his task—a race to the finish. The renewed energy will last for a while, but again he will begin to flag. However, as the end nears, the anticipation of completing the project will energize him. This will sustain him until he actually puts the final touch on his activity. Upon applying this final touch, there will be a moment when his desire is fulfilled and gives way to joy. This elation, this sense of well–being, is the emotional end that accompanies the completion of his work. Note well this wonderful sense of joy felt when a work is brought to completion.

We can see, then, that the emotions of a craftsman flow up and down through his making, much like hills and valleys in the countryside. He starts out high with the anticipatory joy of the final end, flags down as he tires, rises a bit in anticipation of the midpoint reached, again dips as he labors towards the end, but once more begins to swell as he approaches nearer to the completion—and bursts into joy as he reaches the end.

Chapter Six

The Modern Factory Lacks a Beginning, Middle, and End

We have seen that the normal procedure in making something is to have an idea of it first and then to begin a series of steps to accomplish it with a definite beginning, middle, and end. Let us turn our attention now to most processes in manufacturing today. We will consider manufacturing because it is the field where it is easiest to see our point, but all the same concepts can be applied to secretarial work, accounting, nursing, teaching, and just about every other work environment to some degree or another.

The processes of manufacturing are set forth in the discussion of the division of labor concept worked out in the eighteenth century, primarily by Adam Smith. To paraphrase and summarize: one person does one task and one motion, which leads to increased skill, increased speed, less re-working, exact copies, increased productivity per worker, increased production for the whole plant, faster work, lower expenses, and higher yields.

Let's take the making of a table as an example and illustrate the difference between how the table would be made in the days of old as opposed to how it would be made today.

In the old days, there was one craftsman, one shop, many tools, and many different activities.

First, the craftsman selected the appropriate kind of wood, based on the style of the table. Next, the carpenter determined which part of the table he wished to fashion. If he started with the legs, then he had to carry the wood to the appropriate workbench, measure and cut it, and then turn the leg on a lathe. The end of the leg had to be shaped to properly fit the tabletop. Wood for the top had to be carried to this or another workbench, measured, cut, sanded, and drilled with holes that would accept pegs for attaching the legs. Glue had to be sought. Clamps had to be applied to hold the parts together while gluing.

Every step required a new tool, and there was a lot of movement of the wood from place to place. This craftsman had to be skilled at many activities: measuring, cutting, gluing, lengthening, drilling, hammering, clamping, sanding, assembling, and so on.

Today, there is one man, one tool, one shop or cell, and one activity. The one activity is to make one part of the final product. The one man makes for example, only a table leg. This he does over and over. The table is made through a series of steps originating from different cells. Each part is made in a different cell.

A material handler brings a piece of wood to the first worker, who puts it on a template and cuts it to length. He passes it by handcart or conveyor to the next man, who puts it in the lathe and lathes the legs. He removes it, and it moves on to the next station. The next person shapes and fastens the legs to fit into the tabletop. He finishes it, and it's passed on to the next man, who drills holes in the end. There are men making the tabletop along the same lines, each worker doing a small task. The drilling, sanding, and shaping are all done by different workers as the parts are passed down the line. Each time the worker finishes his task, he passes it down the line, picks up another part that was passed to him, and repeats his same activity again. Eventually, all these parts make it to a rendezvous point where workers are tasked to assemble the parts into the table.

Whereas the craftsman of old was able to make the formed legs for one table in four days, the modern factory worker might make fifty legs in one day. The legs would be almost identical as the workman's skill progresses. Since he has only one distinct task to perform, he would use fewer tools. Consequently, he becomes very efficient.

We can observe a difference between an artist who performs all the tasks necessary to complete the final object and this workman who does only one task of many. This workman, depending on how far the job is broken down, does just one task—for example, making table legs. Or if the process is broken down into smaller steps, the worker is only responsible for drilling four holes in the table.

The worker who fashions the whole leg is closer to the artist of old than the driller is. He can still see the leg as being part of the whole even though he will not participate in the completion of the table. The leg becomes his whole sculpture. This worker doesn't see or picture the table as the end of his activity. The chair leg becomes his whole project—whereas, the man drilling only the holes is even further removed from any sense of the end: the whole product. His beginning, middle, and end are simply reduced to drilling four holes, which can hardly be seen as the part of any whole. The more the different steps of the process are broken down, the further removed a worker becomes from having any sense of the whole object. His activity is reduced to mere repetitious acts. This lends itself to mechanization as machines become more refined and the motion becomes more simple and repetitious. And so the workman is reduced to performing a robotic motion with very little difference between the beginning and end of his activity.

Working in this way has a very deleterious effect on the workers emotions. In particular, there are two negative emotional aspects of the monotonous activity that the assembly line and division of labor induces. First, the worker has little if any satisfaction in the final product.

He has only made a small part of it and doesn't see it finished. He doesn't have a chance to reap the joy of being involved in the final touch of the artifact. In most cases, the final product is so removed from him that he never sees it before it is shipped away. This worker has put as much physical and emotional effort into his work to get his part completed as the traditional craftsman, but this worker is left with no emotional pleasure as a reward for his labors. The lack of this joy leads to frustration and anger and its unhealthy consequences.

Second, the more his work is reduced to repetition, the more bored the worker becomes. As we can all attest, boredom drags the soul down, resulting in restlessness, melancholy, or some other negative emotion. Robotic action is not natural to man's creative spirit, and all men chafe under the yoke of never-ending drudgery. Drilling four holes in a table leg over and over is just this—drudgery. It is as if one is stuck in a no-man's land of a continuous middle, an activity without approach to an end. The word end here means the final object, as for example, the finished table, the fashioned statue, the complete computer, or the finished automobile.

We noticed before in our discussion concerning one's emotions that there are times, usually between the beginning and the middle and then again between the middle and the end of making, when there is a sort of dogged determination to get to an endpoint. This is when the emotions of anticipation, expectant joy, and the like are at their lowest. An intense but unsatisfying effort is made to get through the tedious and boring part of a project. This is where it is not very evident that the project is coming into being. For example, a man must turn a lot of excess wood away on the lathe before his table leg begins to take shape. A sculptor must chisel away a lot of excess marble around a certain part of his statue before he can really get to shape an arm or a head. The shoemaker must sew heavy thread around a whole sole, painstakingly and slowly, before his shoe is complete. What re-arouses the higher emotions is when the material begins to unfold into the desired object.

What we can see from this is that, as the whole process ceases to be the work of one man, each smaller process begins to look like the least pleasurable aspect of the artisan's work. When the carpenter of old had to sand his wood, it was a long and tedious task, but it could obviously be seen as a part of a larger picture. This is when he feels a dogged determination. He anticipated getting out of this emotion as he neared the end because he could see that the sanding fit into the whole picture. This is unlike the worker whose task of sanding is separated from all the other tasks. All he does is sand. After he sands a part, he passes it on and begins to sand another. There is a disconnect between himself and the whole table. His emotion largely remains at the stage of dogged determination because he has no sense of completing a whole.

No man can remain in that state. He begins to look

for a change, for excitement, for some other emotion. He becomes disgruntled and grumbles about the monotony of his life. Viewed on a larger scale, since he lives in a society where most goods are made in this way, his standard of living is much higher. He owns more and better things than his grandparents, but the eight or more hours per day he spends at work are less satisfying and infect the rest of his outlook on life.

Chapter Seven

The Assembly Line

ALTHOUGH there are many advantages for a company to use the assembly line it remains a spirit-killer for the workers. This assembly line aspect of a job often leads to a lack of productivity. The whole justification for using the assembly line is to increase productivity—and indeed it does so. But there is an effect on the workers that lessens the impact of the efficiency that was gained by the assembly line method. The reason for this is that every person is an artist of some kind. Every work takes some skill or art. Everyone approaches their task as having a beginning, middle, and an end. Everyone goes through the emotions that accompany the carrying out of their work. When the work is simply adding one thing to a box and pulling another thing out of a different box, the worker becomes a zombie and resigns himself to drudgery. His work literally has no end in sight, and so there is no anticipated joy. This is why even when statistics look good concerning output, all the employees remain unhappy.

Most of these employees are adults who need to have

jobs. They find ways of disciplining themselves to accept the dispiriting aspects of their work and try to adjust to them. They will do what is necessary, but they do it with a lot of resentment. Bosses often cannot understand why there is such discontent; they wonder what could be so wrong.

The problem lies in the lack of an end, or purpose, for the employees. This is the lack of seeing an anticipated end, the chance to rest for a moment and enjoy the task's completion. The conveyor belt is the quintessential example of having no end. It's a nifty invention to get goods from one place to another. But when a worker works on one, it's like floating in the middle of an unending task. When the worker looks one way, he sees a long line of goods coming at him from either a long way away or from a hole in a dividing wall; and when the worker looks the other way, that long belt extends out of sight. To accomplish anything seems hopeless.

I myself floated for months on a fish-gutting line in a southeast Alaskan fishery. The cleaning line was set up as follows: At the beginning of a very long conveyor belt was a hopper that could hold hundreds of fish. This hopper, which was never allowed to go empty, was filled by a man unloading fish from trucks. On the other end of the conveyor belt stood inspectors, grading the fish as they came off the belt and tossing them into their proper totes. Dozens of workers lined each side of the belt. Each had to do one short, quick cleaning task on the fish as it passed in front of him. The conveyor never stopped moving. As I stood and worked, there seemed to be an endless line of fish coming at me from my left. After I picked up a fish, did my part to clean it, and replaced it on the belt, it rejoined a long stream of fish that would disappear into a washer, from which they emerged to be sorted by the inspectors. What an incentive killer this setup was! All of us workers were lost in a sea of fish. We never saw the hopper go empty at the beginning of the belt, and so we never had the satisfaction of any kind of completion. We also never saw the totes fill up at the end of the belt, as they were always removed before they got full. Consequently, we never saw an end to that effort either. Many find themselves in similar situations in other workplaces, and they all experience the same emotions.

Consider a secretary who sorts and answers mail all day. She has an inbox and an outbox. She starts with the inbox. It has x number of packages in it. As she sets about her task, it seems to have an end. But, no; more packages are added before her inbox is emptied—very frustrating! If too much mail piles up and she cannot see an end, her mood plummets. Her work-pace slows. Her efficiency is shot. She tells herself that there is always tomorrow, so she might as well get caught up then. What she means by caught up is important here. She means an end to the task of emptying the inbox. It's okay if it is filled again, but not until it is emptied! It must be emptied by her, and joy must be felt at the accomplishment before more mail is added to her inbox.

These examples provide important clues to help us discover solutions to eliminate disincentives at work. How can we maximize work and productivity and apply incentives that augment the natural emotions of the worker as he sets about his work? First and foremost, we can see that adding the sense of a beginning, middle, and end to a task is critical.

Every person who examines his daily work can discover whether his series of tasks mimics those of the craftsman or if his tasks are more like those of the assembly line worker. By imagining a spectrum where one end is the archetypical craftsman and the other extreme is the assembly line worker, he should have a fair sense of where to place his work. The extent to which one is happy and satisfied with his job can usually be determined by where he lies on this spectrum. The more he lies toward the assembly line side, the more he falls into the drudge, slave mentality. The more he lies to the craftsman side, the more he enjoys his labor and views himself as a creator or master.

The challenge is to make the assembly line worker as pleased with his work as the craftsman. How can we set up this situation within the process of work itself? Could we add a visual aid that would give the drudge a sense of beginning, middle, and end? This visual aid could be a definable and pleasing object to marvel at. The aid could imitate the situation of the artist.

It is of utmost importance to imitate the situation of the artist. Before we go into detail on how we can implement this imitation, let us examine further circumstances that discourage the modern worker in his work. Thus we can have a fuller picture of what distresses an employee. In this way, when we come up with our solutions, we can see how they will mitigate the major incentive killers in the workplace.

Chapter Eight

Utility and Beauty

ONE aspect of man's nature that induces him to work and connects him emotionally to it is his desire to fashion something not only functional, but beautiful as well. There are those arts—we generally refer to them as fine arts—that are devoted exclusively to allowing men to delight in a thing on account of its beauty alone. But there are also arts designed to the making of useful things, such as door latches. These are things not made for their own sake, but only to be used for something else like holding a door closed. Typically, the primary concern of the craftsman is not to make a door latch that looks good. Rather, his primary intention is to craft it so that it holds a door shut. Likewise, a hatchet is made for chopping; a tractor to pull things; a warehouse to store things; a computer to compute. The arts that go into making these things are called practical arts. These arts exist because they are required to make things to be used. The art used in making them is only around as long as there is a need for such products. The slide rule used to be made by artisans but not any longer. We have a new tool to do this work—the calculator.

If we consider the useful objects of the past, we find it remarkable that most were made beautiful as well. Granted, there is a kind of simple beauty in any object that has a use, and of course the level of beauty varies from object to object. But this is not the beauty I am primarily concerned with here. Rather, I am referring to the added embellishment that the craftsman added to his work to make it pleasing to the eye. One could say many things concerning the "why" of this phenomenon—namely, why a man wishes even his most practical things to have beauty. Suffice it to say, this is a commonly observed occurrence and a very important one. The embellishments on such menial objects add an even greater satisfaction to a craftsman's work than just the mere completion of it. A double satisfaction is enjoyed.

Consider the fancy door hinges that were found on barns and houses, the fancy carriages, the gingerbread trim on houses, the shaped knife handles, and the filigree on boots. All of these ornate objects were clearly made for use; yet they would work equally well without any embellishment—in some cases they would work better. But there is an added delight in one's work when it results not only in a useful thing but in one of beauty as well. This added delight is an added incentive both to begin the work in the first place and to continue the work once it has started.

There are four reasons why we have lost this sense of beauty in our workmanship. The first reason has to do with the loss of the sense of beauty in general. This flows from a philosophical difference in how man views his place in the universe now as compared to then.

The other three reasons are directly linked to the worker. The second reason is that machines have become much more complex and many of their parts are hidden from the eye. The third is that the division of labor has become more refined, and it is less obvious to the individual worker where each part fits into the whole.

Indeed, many assembly line jobs are done by people who have little idea of how the parts they are working on will actually be used in the final product. Most of the workers do not need to have any knowledge of the final product. A person who inspects a small piece of metal for defects never needs to know its function in order to be a good inspector. Someone punching holes in a piece of steel needs to know only a few things about the piece he is working on. Consequently, the beauty of the final product is not apparent to him at all. As machines become more complex, each piece is less relatable to the whole. For example, a rifle made in the eighteenth century had few moving parts, and all of its parts were visible. The hammer, the barrel, and the stock could all be embellished by shaping or engraving. The rifle could be made to be both functional and very pleasing artistically as well. In contrast, if we consider a sophisticated gun on a modern battleship, there are quite a few parts to it, to say the least. It employs recoil, cooling, and loading; it is computer-driven, and most of its parts are unseen. Consequently, there is no motivation to make the gun beautiful. Often the whole gun is hidden and therefore clearly needs no embellishment.

The last reason is, not surprising, cost. In modern times, we have moved ever closer toward use and profit; consequently, beauty has taken a backseat. Embellishment could be added at an increased cost, but to stay in business these days, a manufacturer must compete for customers through lower prices and higher quality. Still, the customer does have some control over the retreat from beauty caused by today's competitive environment. He can take control by avoiding the purchase of objects that have no aesthetic appeal.

In sum, the disappearance of beauty from the utilitarian arts and the consequent removal of incentive to do work results from the following:

- The philosophical outlook on life that discards the beautiful for the sake of the useful is becoming more prevalent
- The parts one is making become less visible as the machine being made becomes more and more complicated
- The division of labor is broken down more and more, so that each worker sees less of the

final product and its possibilities for beautiful embellishment
- The costs have become too high to embellish a purely utilitarian product when a company must compete to have the best price.

Chapter Nine

Rhythm

THE process of making an object can be seen as a kind of rhythm—a flow of energy from the maker into the work. It ebbs and flows as the activity unfolds, and there are emotions that rise and fall accordingly as the work progresses. It is in taking advantage of these emotions that the well-designed incentive program can best be utilized. At each step, there are anticipations, frustrations, and small delights of relief as obstacles are overcome. Mistakes are rectified, and the work materializes. This all forms the rhythm of which I speak, and the artist is prepared to handle all the parts of this rhythm. It's easy to see how important rhythm is in music; it is arguably just as important in any worthwhile work. In fact, it is the breaching of this rhythm, the interrupting of the work that can cause the worker so much frustration. In understanding this frustration and its sources, we can best see how to order our work.

Among the emotions that ebb and flow through the rhythm of work, there is a sense of determination to get through a particular step in a task. Another emotion is the sense of triumph when a particular part of the work is complete. And another is the feeling of delight when a difficult part of the task is accomplished. From this point, the emotions begin to slope down into a sort of doggedness to plow through another part, accompanied by a building anticipation of completion and the subsequent joy. Finally, the whole task reaches completion.

Chapter Ten

Incentives

INCENTIVES are added inducements offered to a person to spur him on to greater action or achievement. Often this takes the form of a bonus of some kind, perhaps a monetary reward, or possibly a plaque, given for outstanding performance.

Those of you who have enjoyed the pleasures of a county fair will recall the delight of the boy who wins the blue ribbon for his prize steer, or the woman who glows on account of her jam being judged the best in the county. The conversations that ensue after the judging are most instructive. There is talk among the contestants of how next year this or that change is going to be made to make their work even better. Or again, for those who enjoy a stout one now and then, recall that in medieval times the lord and the nobility would judge the beer made by housewives, to ensure that the quality of beer in the realm was maintained and improved. They insured this by recognizing and rewarding the best woman's work.

In the modern work-place, incentives are added bonuses given to an employee as an award for accomplishing a certain set of goals. An incentive is something on top of his compensation. Generally, we do not call a worker's paycheck an incentive, although it is why he comes to work in the first place. The paycheck, healthcare, pension, and other benefits the company may offer are considered the worker's just compensation. This is a sort of contract between employer and employee whereby a certain work is done for certain compensation. Incentives, however are added rewards used to increase the productivity of the employee. All other things being equal, incentives are intended to increase the output of the employee beyond what he is normally expected to produce.

In the days when horses were used to pull loads, a trick was sometimes used to keep the horse moving. The wagoner would suspend a carrot in front of the horse's nose to get him to walk. The carrot would be removed, and the horse would stop. The horse would be fed a number of carrots so he would not lose interest in the bait. The carrots he consumed and the care he received would be considered his just compensation. It is what he was owed for his labors. The carrot in front of his nose can be likened to the pay and benefits that the employee receives.

But when the wagoner put sugar or molasses on the carrot, the horse walked faster. The milkman could lengthen his milk route and make more money, and the horse got to eat molasses with his carrot if he performed this extra activity. We could say the horse had an added incentive to increase his activity.

Here's a more modern application. A machinist is expected to turn out twenty pieces a day, give or take three or four depending on other variables. He is compensated for this effort through his pay and benefits. When his supervisor wants the machinist to make an extra effort to turn out twenty-five pieces a day, he may offer an incentive. Perhaps, if the machinist meets the goal of twenty-five pieces a day for two weeks, he will receive a twenty-five dollar gift certificate to the nearest steakhouse. Now this bonus becomes an added incentive for the machinist, and is contingent on the worker accomplishing a goal over and above what is ordinarily expected of him.

This kind of incentive is quite effective and certainly has its place in the arsenal of the supervisor. But we must note that this kind of incentive does not change anything in respect to the beginning, middle, and end of the craftsman's activity. It also is not tied directly to the emotions that naturally follow the machinist's work. This kind of incentive is one that appeals to him because of what he can do with the reward in his life outside of the workplace. The certificate can be spent for some good, and therefore he will want to work harder to attain that good.

However, in this case, the supervisor has not enhanced the worker's job satisfaction. The repetitiveness and the workers inability to see the finished product still remain the same. The increased productivity of the worker can only be sustained for so long until he gets burned out. The reality of his tedium will again sink in.

Another kind of incentive is the praise given by the boss throughout the day or week. This incentive appeals to the desire to be recognized and appreciated by others. This is a very powerful incentive, and increases job satisfaction. A pat on the back by the boss and a sincere good job for a job well done fills the employee with pride and spurs him on to greater achievement. But this incentive only reaches its apex if it is aligned with the joy that a worker is feeling when he has just completed his work. As we saw in our previous discussion concerning the emotions of the craftsman: his crowning emotion was the joy accompanying the completion of his work.

There is a natural desire to share this joy with others. The occasion to share such joy is not always possible, but the desire to do so is universally felt. There is a social aspect to this joy that begs emphasis. Joy is one of those emotions that, if shared, is augmented in the person feeling it. This desire to share joy may be mistaken for the simple desire to be recognized. A desire to be recognized does play a large part in the creative process, nevertheless for the person who wants to be recognized for what he has done, it is crucial that he thinks that the people recognizing him for his achievement share in his joy. If the reward of joy stays only with the craftsman, it lacks much of the motivational quality necessary to launch him energetically into his next task.

This need to share joy with others is essential to the thesis I am proposing: The optimization of this need to share joy will make all incentive programs work better. It is when this joy is felt that a reward should be offered for the job done.

Incentives are added bonuses given to an employee as an award for accomplishing a certain set of goals. Almost every incentive plan fails to achieve its full effect because of its failure to align the reward with the joy one feels when his work is accomplished. Most plans act too late to capitalize on this moment, and therefore, they fail to be a motivator of any significance for the worker.

Another kind of incentive is to increase competition among employees, although one must know the dispositions of the individuals involved. This is not always possible but can be used to great effect when appropriate. This will be addressed more fully in the chapter on how to apply incentives properly in the workplace.

Year-end bonuses are another possible incentive to offer—if certain goals are reached, certain payouts are made.

As we can see there are many variations on incentive programs, but I believe none addresses the particular problem of tedium on the jobsite.

Chapter Eleven

Ways Incentive Is Killed in the Modern Workplace

Interrupting the Work Flow

A major factor contributing to poor productivity is the effect of interruptions on the employee. These differ greatly from job to job; they depend on how the employee is connected emotionally to his work. If an employee is in a work environment in which he feels he is a craftsman, then interruptions will have an extremely deleterious effect on his productivity. As a craftsman, he goes through all the emotions concomitant with the beginning, middle, and end of his work. To be interrupted during this work is highly frustrating. The concentrated effort necessary to work well requires blocking out all distractions— immersing himself in a world of his own. It takes time to shed the images and feelings he had when he started his work and to flow into this stream of emotions. To be interrupted jolts him from this narrow world and causes his emotions to be cut off from their natural end. This results in a heightened form of the frustration we all feel when we are interrupted.

Contrast this to the employee who is related to his work in the mode of an assembly line worker. He will look forward to any interruption as a way to escape the confines of his activities. In this situation it is the supervisors who feel frustrated when their employees take many bathroom breaks or stand around the coffee machine and talk. Understandably, the employees will do anything to distract themselves from the drudgery to which they must return. This obviously reduces productivity.

Hence, a responsibility of the supervisor is to try to eliminate, or at least mitigate, as much of the slave mentality as possible. He or she does this by putting in place incentives, methods, or environments that will make the worker view himself as a craftsman, not a slave. Removing interruptions that deny him his rhythm of work is a starting point.

An examination of situations where the flow of beginning, middle, and end is interrupted will make this point more clear. Keeping focused on the idea that the whole process, from the picking up of the first tool to the final touch, is one complete activity is critical to our understanding. It is the final end that gives rise to the whole endeavor. It is also critical to remember that an essential aspect of a task is the joy that accompanies its completion

Let's start with a situation where an activity is interrupted from flowing to its natural completion. In this example, an employee is in a state of joy after having accomplished a task, but his boss suggests that some further output would be desirable. This is a situation where not only is the moment of joy not used as a moment of reward and further incentive, but it is actually destroyed. This causes the worker to resent his work, and it actually diminishes his output.

Assume that Jane has seventeen samples to inspect and package. She sets up her work station and has a definite beginning (seventeen packages), middle (inspect and pack), and end (all are ready to ship) to her work. She can see these both mentally and physically before her. She energetically begins her task and then experiences all the emotions of the work process.

Nearing the end of her task, the seventeen packages have been inspected and packaged and the path of emotions has been traversed. Jane draws to the end of her work and satisfaction ensues. Her boss, aware that she has finished this work, comes and congratulates her, but in the midst of that congratulation says, "You did a wonderful job, thank you. The shipment will now go out. What do you think we could do to improve efficiency and get an eighteenth item out?" Our hapless boss does not realize that he has sown a seed of discontent as he tries to be encouraging. This was not the right thing to say. In the midst of joy, a comment has been infused that implies that

Jane's effort was not good enough. The supervisor failed to take into account that there is a natural time period over which the emotion of joy is felt. If this emotion of fulfillment is interrupted, there is frustration. This is not the time to suggest improvement, as we can see by contrasting the thoughts motivating the boss's speech with what the employee hears.

The boss is thinking, "This worker really worked hard. She took the initiative to get this job done. I really like her can-do attitude. She sets up her work station neatly and sails through her work. I don't know how she gets all this done before it's time to ship. I will give her the thanks she deserves." That he does, but he continues, "If I could get her another piece of equipment that is faster or move her work station, she might then be able to get an eighteenth item out, or more. I know these suggestions might work, but she would be the one to ask. If she could come up with some ideas and we could get them implemented, I'll be able to meet my goals and get a raise or promotion, and she will be even more valuable to the company."

From our vantage point, seeing the supervisor's thoughts, we see how harmless his comment is and how very flattering. We must remember, though, that the only words he really said to her were, "What do you think we could do to improve efficiency?"

She hears, "What you just did is not quite good enough. You failed. We may have to look at other ways of getting this done." Just at the point when she feels most elated, she hears that she is not good enough.

The setup, the anticipation of the job being completed, the determination to get the job done, and all the hours she worked as she went up and down in emotion through the whole process of beginning, middle, and end is all for naught. She thinks she is not appreciated or recognized, and more importantly, in the midst of her feeling of joy, she is robbed of it. Instead of a shared joy, she perceives negativity. What might be her reaction when the next seventeen items must be rushed out to shipment? The emotion she was left with after her former effort was resentment of the boss and thoughts of, "How dare he ask for more."

We can see that she takes his question of improvement personally. She is not thinking along the same line as he is. She feels inadequate. She does not know all the thoughts that were in the mind of the boss. She does not think that having inadequate equipment might have an influence on the speed or efficiency of her work, even though that is what the boss is thinking. He is shocked at the negative feelings and resentment he's getting from her. He doesn't recognize that, while feeling joy, she wants only praise or reward and for others to share her joy. He doesn't see that he must let the natural flow of emotion play out and be resolved. Jane prides herself on her work, and she feels she has put as much effort into the task as possible. When the supervisor's question comes, she resents it because she thinks the whole concept of getting it done faster is absurd.

If the boss were asked, "Did you communicate to your employees that we need improvement in our packaging unit? That we must really get eighteen or more items out?", in all honesty, he could say yes. He did say those words, and they were true. Jane did get the message that more must be done. But it was at the cost of resentment. The timing and approach were wrong. This happens when the end emotion is interrupted.

The same negative effect is felt at every step of the process when one is interrupted. Anger and resentment are felt when having to stop whatever emotion one is in. The proper way to handle this situation would be to separate the praise and joy of the employee from the request for improvement. This would satisfy both the employee and supervisor. The praise would be given at the joyful time, which would be highly appreciated by the employee. The time for a discussion of improvement would be at a different time, preferably away from the work station.

The idea is to separate the personal part of the improvement from the improvement of the process. In this case, the boss could discuss with Jane how a piece of new equipment might increase production and ease her work. Or how a rearrangement of the work area would enhance the same, and then he might proceed with examples of where this has succeeded before. Thus her work would be uninterrupted and would be allowed to reach its natural end. This would ensure efficiency and satisfaction and leave her disposed to the possibilities of improvement in due time.

We all have been interrupted in our work. We feel a sense of anger that might manifest itself as either only a mere touch of annoyance or as an outburst of emotion. Why such an emotional response? A machine does not react this way; it is turned off and turned on and never knows the difference. A person, though, reacts much differently. This is because at every step of the way, he is concentrating on a particular step in his process and there is a particular emotion connected to that moment. When interrupted, that emotion is stopped dead in its tracks. There is no completion—hence, frustration.

If a worker is in a determined state of mind and is interrupted, it is as if that emotion is wasted, and he must start all over. He must return to the most distasteful part of his task right when he was beginning to delight in the anticipated joy of completing it. When his momentum increases as he draws closer to this final joy but is then interrupted, he feels robbed of the joy. And again, he has to start all over in his emotion.

If a man is taken away from his task altogether, he can adjust to his new activity. But when he simply returns to his initial task, he must readjust his thinking. He must visualize where he was in the creation process and then readjust his emotions to where they were when he was interrupted. It takes time and effort to do this.

We can illustrate this by a scene we are all familiar with. A man is immersed in his work and gets a phone call—maybe even just a two-minute call. When the phone rings, he leaves his work with some exasperation. After he services the call, he rejoins his work where he left off. Right when he has absorbed himself again in his work, the phone jars him from his concentration, and this time he responds with greater exasperation. When this sequence repeats itself again, he responds with an expletive and throws down his tools in anger. Yes, even if he has the responsibility of taking a phone call as part of his job description, he still reacts with anger when the call intrudes on him. For every time he is interrupted and then returns to his work, he must readjust himself emotionally back into it.

This man's boss may make a time study to see how much time is necessary to take this man's product from beginning to end. He may then wonder why it has taken this worker so much longer to accomplish his task than the process demands. When the employee is confronted with this fact, the employee smarts back that if he didn't have so many interruptions, he would be done in a much timelier manner. The boss looks at the phone log and sees there were only three short phone calls on that day.

This shows that the lost time is not really equal to the lost productivity. What the boss doesn't understand is that every time the worker's rhythm is broken, there is a much longer delay than the actual phone call. The worker spends considerable time readjusting himself emotionally to the rhythm of his work.

The Fear of Change

Another aspect that hinders the effectiveness of incentives is the fear of change. In some people, this is a very real and powerful motivation not to improve.

When we examine the fear of change, we can see that it's not really fear of change in general that a person is apprehensive about but fear of a few particular changes. It is not really change that is feared but only specific changes that aren't desired. The change of a worker's wage is a good example. A higher wage is desired, eagerly anticipated, and eagerly embraced. A lower wage is feared and, if possible, rejected. Similarly, a promotion is a big change, but anticipated with joy; the change of demotion is also a big change, but is feared. So, really, it's not change we fear but the bad things we anticipate that might come about when the change takes place.

Usually in these cases, employees are aware of their fears, but often they won't tell anyone for further fear of embarrassment or retribution. One fear that is very common is the fear that a particular change will force us to work harder. Lethargy may be the answer to that fear, but even when it is not and there is justification for the change, a change that may increase an employee's work load is viewed with suspicion.

Although it is difficult to discern all the reasons why

workers resist change in the work place, there are two causes that can be addressed here, for they fall under our purview of the worker and his emotional habits. The first reason workers resist change is that a man works by habit and habits resist change; the second reason is that the worker usually believes that his way of doing his job is best.

The first cause for resisting change is quite reasonable, because any time we must break a habit and form a new one, it requires greater concentration and more intense work. It is hard work, for a time, to learn a new habit. So the worker's fear that he will have to work harder is true, but if the change is for the better, the pain will only last until the new habit is acquired, and then the new way of doing things becomes commonplace. So, although the fear is real, it is often exaggerated in the employee's mind.

The second cause for resisting change is also reasonable. No one purposely sets about a task with the intent of doing it in the hardest way. Indeed, everybody will try to do the task in the easiest way. So the proposal to change the approach is met with skepticism.

Closely linked to the fear of having to work harder is the fear that one will have to work longer. The concept is not so scary in itself, but it is connected to other activities the employee is involved in outside of work. As soon as an employee thinks that the change is going to affect his outside activities, he balks. He sees a concrete thing being missed. For some, it's meeting buddies after work to go fishing, for others, it's hitting the gym. For still others, it's picking their kids up at a particular time. The examples are as numerous as there are people. Working longer always cuts into other activities, and the worker fears this loss.

Another powerful fear that arises, of course, is the fear that if a worker's job can be made more efficient through improvements in the process or by the introduction of machines, the worker will no longer be needed. For example, if there are ten machinists working in a shop and someone says, "Hey, we can make each of you so efficient that each of you can do the same amount of work in half the time," they really might be saying that they need only five of the workers to do the same amount of work. If, in fact, the company continued to sell the same number of parts, then five machinists would have to be laid off to cut the cost of labor. For an expanding company, this simply means that the company can sell twice the parts and increase their profit. So this is a real fear that an employee can have when change is introduced. He wonders which one of his fellow employees is expendable. It doesn't help to tell him that only the five worst machinists will be the ones to go or to be the best and not to worry. These statements may all be true—it is in the best interest of the company to keep the best employees. It is also true that the employees will have to compete to keep their jobs. Unfortunately, this motivation only works for the competitive and confident employees—it results in fear and resentment for the rest.

Reworking

Reworking poses an especially difficult challenge in the work-place. A worker resists reworking because he has already gone through the emotional roller coaster in fashioning a product. To hold onto an object that is already complete but defective is discouraging, not only because the worker is denied the pleasure of seeing the finished product, but also because all of his effort and emotion appear wasted. This robs the worker of joy and renders his past activities void. Of course, one can learn from mistakes, but at the moment of recognition of a failed effort, there is only disappointment.

There are two possible sequels to a failure of this kind. Either a worker reworks his part of a product to make it usable, or he scraps it and begins a whole new work. If one begins anew, there is no recovery of the energy spent in making the original item. In reworking it, there can at least be a partial recovery of efforts already made. However, the same enthusiasm is required when he must rework a part as when he made the original. This is extremely difficult. There is usually no energy left to go down that path again. Even when one's work entails making dozens or hundreds of the same object, a worker would rather start on a new object than rework an existing one.

Having expended his effort upon the part, a worker is more willing to move on to another part and start the whole process again. He isn't willing to expend energy to go over old ground to fix a part he failed in making right the first time. Obviously, in most cases in business, it makes monetary sense to rework a defective part, but an observable phenomenon in the workplace is the reluctance or even anger that is involved when one has to rework something. The normal desire is to move on, to start with the next process. One possible solution to this is to designate a particular person to rework defective parts. This person will not yet have expended any emotion or effort on an unfinished object, so he has not felt any disappointment over the failed part. He can approach that part as a different kind of work. He can picture in his mind how the part is to look and set about his task just like the man starting with raw material. The difference is that the repairer's materials already have much of the final form imprinted in them, but his work will still have a beginning, middle, and end and all their consequent emotions.

Reworking is necessary in business because no process is ever perfect. We mention this, to illustrate once again the reluctance one feels in working with an interrupted rhythm. When this natural rhythm of the craftsman is interrupted, it brings about an emotional discomfort that leads to unhappy workers. Consequently, production slows. A machine that makes a part over and over and makes one defective obviously could not care less if the defective part has to be fed back through. But a human being that has to rework an object is doing work he has already completed and, therefore, resents the interruption.

Chapter Twelve

Solutions

Inventing a Beginning, Middle, and End

IT is necessary here to propose solutions to the difficulties that specialization and assembly-line work have produced in our workplace. These solutions will enable the modern worker to get the same satisfaction from work that the artist or craftsman enjoys. How will we achieve such solutions? Supervisors will need to provide a visible means of indicating a beginning, middle, and end to their employees' work.

We cannot stress enough the importance of having a definite beginning, middle and end. If the task does not have an obvious beginning, middle, and end, a worker will try to invent them. A wonderful example comes from my older brother's experience as an employee on a potato farm in Washington state. He was about fifteen years old, and a farmer needed seed potatoes cut into chunks with the right number of eyes on them. My brother, two of our sisters, and sometimes a few others were required to pick a potato out of a tote on their left, examine it, cut it into pieces, and then toss it into a tote sitting at their right.

The full tote on their left was the beginning of their task. This tote half empty was the middle. And the empty tote was the end. This single tote gave them a very visible, and therefore intuitively measurable, way to see the progress of their work. An added way this beginning, middle, and end were realized was by watching the tote on their right fill up. There was always a shared joy and sigh of relief as the farmer removed the full tote and a fresh tote was put into its place. The process of fully filling the next tote then started.

Furthermore, on this farm, there were no incentives to get a certain number of totes filled, as the workers were getting paid hourly only. Despite this, if a break was coming or lunchtime was approaching, something very beneficial for the farmer happened. If it was not impossible to fill the tote before that break, a frenzy of activity would ensue to get that tote filled before the break was announced. Smiles and a feeling of satisfaction for having finished the tote before lunch were enjoyed by all. Notice that the goal of filling this tote before lunch took no instigation from the farmer. When it happened, the task was accomplished, and with relief, they got up for break. Even if they weren't able to accomplish their goal, it was a plus for the farmer, for that last flurry of activity filled his tote faster. And all this was at no cost to him. It was human nature to set about completing a task that needed to be done. This natural flow of emotion happens when a person has a visual, or at least measurable, beginning, middle, and end to his work. In this case, it resulted in increased productivity for the farmer at no added cost.

But when the farmer tried to improve the situation, something happened that deflated the enthusiastic employees. The farmer thought that time could be saved and more work would be done if the tote that was being filled was replaced before it got full. The concept was to avoid the small break the workers got when waiting for the new tote. Presumably, this would allow the workers to continuously turn out potatoes until the next official break. The actual effect it had was the opposite of the one desired. The workers slowed down to a sluggish plod. By the end of the day, their enthusiasm left and there was grumbling. The farmer's thought had seemed valid—remove slack time and increase efficiency. But the farmer overlooked the human factor. What was being taken away was any sense of a beginning, middle, and end to the work. To the workers, it now looked like a continuous stream of labor with no definable end. This led to a kind of hopelessness, and the work became drudgery. The workers slipped into the slave mentality and gave a mediocre effort. The slowdown was noticeable.

Similar scenes are played out across the whole labor spectrum. A few more examples will be helpful, as seeing this principle in action is crucial in devising proper remedies. One example comes from my experience working in a metal-analyzing lab for many years.

A small sample of material would be sent to the lab

to be analyzed for impurities or constituents. The samples arrived at different times during the day and were dropped off at the separate workstations in boxes for the appropriate analyst. When the analyst would come in to begin his shift, he would arrange his samples in a certain order to facilitate the most efficient way to get them all analyzed. He would determine which samples would dissolve faster than the others and which ones had different requirements. He had a certain number of samples in front of him. Like all human endeavors, he visualized a beginning, middle, and end of his work, along with where in that order he should be throughout the day. He would begin to get into the flow of his work—the rhythm that we spoke of before. Barring any interruptions, he would flow through the day in a good mood and go through all the emotions of completing work. However, more samples would invariably be entered into his inbox throughout the day. The reaction of the analyst when this happened (myself included) was one of anger, frustration, and a sense of hopelessness. Questions arose, such as, "Why didn't they get that to us first thing in the morning? Now I have to stop what I'm doing and slide this into the work stream"; or, "Now I'll never get this done. I was hoping to finish completely today"; or, "I just did that kind of test, and now they bring us another one."

All of us reacted with resentment and anger, even though the added samples were within our job description. There was nothing inappropriate about the customers dropping off the samples as they did. From the vantage of logic and efficiency on paper, it was a very good arrangement. But again in this case, the analyst, although having many different kinds of samples to run, used the contents of his inbox as the measure of his task. When he entered in the morning, he began his work by sorting his samples and putting them in order. His goal was to have an empty box at the end of the day. He anticipated the ups and downs of the flow of his work and set about his task. If unimpeded in this task, he had a great sense of accomplishment and well-being when he emptied the box.

The full box was the beginning, the box half-empty was the middle, and the empty box was the end. When additional samples were put into his box, it created tension for two reasons. First, the worker's rhythm was interrupted, and second, the beginning, middle, and end had changed midstream—the end was extended to an indefinable time. Some adjustment could be made, but anger and resentment were present in everyone when their task was altered in this way.

Some people can adjust more readily to change than others, but everyone will feel the tension and will feel a little less happy. If the beginning, middle, and end are changed too much or too often, a feeling of hopelessness sets in and a person's energy gets sapped. He often will express his anger and resentment by becoming depressed and reverting to a plodding pace. This is obviously a detriment to productivity and employee engagement.

The most natural way to provide a beginning, middle, and end is to use the artificial boundaries that boxes or containers provide. An example of this is when a worker receives a certain number of parts to package in an engine parts factory. Let's say the factory from where the parts come works twenty-four hours a day, but the packager only works for eight hours. There will be a certain number of parts sitting in the packager's bin when he arrives in the morning. The engine parts are lined up starting from the front of the bin going to the back side of the bin. Regardless of the actual work that must be done to package each of the parts, there exists an actual beginning, middle, and end of the packager's work for the day. He has a visible means of seeing how much work he has accomplished as the day progresses. He can see when he is halfway finished, and he can see when he is completely finished.

What I have just described to you can be applied to any situation where parts come to a worker on carts. The amount of work has a visible beginning, middle, and end. Mail that comes in the company's mailbox and needs to be opened is usually sorted in piles or bins. These containers provide an artificial beginning, middle, and end.

Most workers will use these situations to measure the progress of their work. When the thing we are working on becomes less an object of art, like the construction of a house, and more an indefinable object, like parts that just keep coming in and going out, our artistic inclination provides an artificial set of boundaries so that we can measure our progress against some foreseeable and definitive end. These artificial boundaries are provided by containers. Sometimes as we approach our work even this set of boundaries which containers provide does not exist. It is up to the supervisors, then, to come up with a way to provide this.

In our earlier example of the workers in the potato line, the farmer made the mistake of removing the natural boundaries of the totes. When these boundaries were removed, it seemed as if the potatoes were coming at the workers in a continuous stream. This is where it would have been better to leave the tote system—as it was with a natural visual boundary.

As far as building space and machinery goes, it may actually be more efficient to use the conveyor system, but an employer will not reap the full benefit of increased productivity because his workers will be deprived of any sense of an end to their work. It is necessary that, along with the change in the workplace, an employer adds a beginning, middle, and end.

In a conveyor system, lines could be drawn every so many feet and numbers assigned to each section. The worker would see the sections as they go by. This would give a sense of division to what seems like a continuous stream. It would also provide the possibility of using each one of the sections as a building block of a virtual house. Each section of the marked belt would count as one brick. As the bricks are built, they could be stacked in virtual bundles. When a certain number of bundles are made, they would be assembled into a virtual house—thus providing a visual beginning, middle, and end. What this also would provide is a discrete way to tie the more traditional means of incentives into the process. For example, the virtual bundles of bricks that are made could be counted. Past data could be used to determine the expected average number of bundles under normal conditions. The supervisor could offer a gift certificate to the employees if they exceeded this number in a given day. Another incentive could be awarded if the whole house were completed within a certain amount of time. A model house to build would provide a visible beginning to one's work each day. It would provide for a certain general idea of when one would reach the halfway point, and it would provide a definite and visible end to the worker's effort.

Once boundaries have been defined in employees' minds, one employer can then apply the more traditional incentives to the work.

Using Virtual Reality

A way of accomplishing the program outlined above would be to have an artifact built virtually along with the actual work being accomplished by the worker.

For example, virtual reality could be introduced into the workplace by setting up an assembly line so that as parts went by the worker, every tenth part that is processed would add a brick to a large virtual house. The virtual house would be shown on a big computer screen on the wall, or better yet, when the technology arrives, a three-dimensional virtual house along the lines of a hologram. The employee could watch the house being built as the day progresses. The construction of the house would be the result of the worker's effort, just as the completion of the actual task would be. When the house was completely built, it would be visible for all to see. He would have been able to see the beginning, middle, and end of his virtual task. The construction of the house would not be of any worth to him as such, but it would be a way of distracting him from his drudgery by giving his work a tangible beginning, middle, and end—providing him with a sense of accomplishment. As we will see in other examples, even this artificial means will lift his spirits.

The vital objective here is to replicate the emotions of the craftsman by introducing elements that mimic the work of the craftsman. Illustration:

Just as the the craftsman who is to construct a table first turns one table leg on a lathe, so too ten groups of ten items that pass by a worker on an assembly line could add up to one wall of a foundation on a house. The craftsman then turns another leg on his lathe; this is like the assembly worker doing another ten of ten for another of his foundation walls. The assembly worker finishing four sides of his foundation is equivalent to the craftsman finishing four legs, As the craftsman shapes the four sides of the top of the table, so the worker raises four walls of his house, and so on.

We can see that we are mimicking the craftsman: just as he works and sees the beginning and middle of his work, so the modern worker now has a visual aid to define how much work he is doing. Other images besides houses could be used ---- anything that has definable boundaries. Again, we must arouse in the worker, whose days are filled with monotony, the emotions natural in man as an artist, by constructing an environment that imitates the world of the craftsman. In this way, a factory worker may share in the natural pleasures that flow from doing a good work. The possibilities for pleasurable virtual projects to pursue are almost endless

The virtual house being built by counting goods processed on a conveyor system lends itself to being built by many workers instead of one, and so, this is an opportune time to introduce the concept of teamwork. So widely is teamwork encouraged throughout industry that it is ubiquitous in the literature and slogans of nearly every company. We are also aware of it from many other venues. How about the glorious barn raising days of our early American heritage? A whole community of craftsmen would gather together and through joint effort would raise a barn in a matter of days—a matter of days as opposed to months,, if one craftsman farmer attempted it alone. Or, the many cowboys it would take to do a round up or cattle drive. All these men would have to work together to bring about a successful drive from Abilene to Chicago or suchlike.

We know that teamwork is an activity performed jointly with two or more individuals who are all dedicated to accomplishing a certain task—the fruit of which they will all enjoy. The use of the barn was not a common good, but the joy felt was. Since this fruit was brought about by the efforts of many and the fruit was shared by all, we can call this fruit a common good. Thus the notion of a common good is introduced as the fruit of teamwork. The efforts of many of the workers are counted separately, but the goods counted are added onto the common house just as the efforts of many craftsmen construct real houses. Thereby through the joint effort of many, the virtual house is constructed. Consequently, the joy of completion of the house is shared, much like the shared joy of the completed pioneer barn.

The joy of the accomplishment is a shared joy and therefore an augmented joy much like the added joy of the craftsman when he can share the joy of his completed statue, table or house.

Further enhancements can be added as incentives to the project of building the house. For instance, the fanciness of the house can be tied to the speed at which the worker is processing parts. This will impart the desire to make the fanciest house possible. And then, the houses that each employee builds must be visible to all, so that images will arouse competition among the employees, much as video games keep track of the highest score. Surely we all have seen the enthusiasm generated from a simple game when players strive to win; we can also harness this competitive spirit to alleviate boring jobs. The uses of competition will be discussed further in chapter fourteen when we further address ways of alleviating monotony, encouraging a beginning middle and end, and increasing output.

Finally, attach monetary rewards to the number and fancifulness of the houses built, and you have the recipe for vastly improving your productivity.

Chapter Thirteen

Maximize Incentive Effectiveness

THE biggest problem with incentive programs is that they do not take advantage of the moment at which a worker needs the incentive. Most incentives are too far removed from day-to-day activity.

For example, let's say a company has an issue related to waste. They have determined that they are losing too much money on wasteful practices. They assemble their twenty employees and propose an incentive plan to motivate their employees to get directly involved with eliminating waste. They present it something like this. In 1995, the company had revenues of $2,000,000. It was determined that after all the overhead and accounting needs were taken care of, there was a $250,000 profit. The company proposes a $500 end-of-the-year bonus for each employee if the amount of money lost on waste is reduced by $70,000. This sounds achievable to the employees. A year to achieve the task seems like a reasonable time frame, and employees are excited as they leave the meeting. However, this incentive is bound to fail. It is too far removed from the employee's everyday work.

Let's consider now one of these employees as he returns from the presentation. His job is to clean a part with a wipe to eliminate excess oil, and he must do this over and over again throughout the day. One wipe at a time would be sufficient. However, when he grabs a wipe from the box, he usually pulls out one or more extra. Every time he cleans a part, the cost of wasted wipes is merely pennies. If we add up all up the waste, it might come to $15 a day. This amount of waste is swallowed by bigger expenses and never noticed.

After the presentation, our employee makes the effort to grab only one wipe at a time, but, he's always in a hurry, and he reasons that one or two wasted wipes is nothing. How could the few pennies make a difference in the $70,000? He reasons that other workers who waste excess oil really make the difference. This worker sees his effort as contributing so little that it is swallowed up and the inconvenience is not worth the cost; so he does nothing. The employees in other departments feel the same way about their waste. The secretaries feel the same way about slow computers or excessive printing and so on. No one has a tangible feel for how each effort could possibly put a dent in the $70,000. The enthusiasm for the incentives ebbs away as old habits take over, and the incentive is forgotten in a matter of days.

Let's look now at how this incentive could work

effectively. The original incentive of saving $70,000 would still be in place, and the $500 bonus check at the end of the year remains a good idea. But to get an individual employee to actually save money at any given time, there must be a tangible reward on a day-to-day or week-to-week basis.

Returning to the employee envisioned above, the wipes he uses in one day could be divided into ten boxes. A goal would then be set that only nine boxes should be used in one day. It will take some innovation and attention by the employee to reach the goal of reducing his ten boxes to nine boxes. Let us assume that this reduction in wipes saves the company $2 a day. For one week, the savings is $20, and after one month it is $80. An incentive could be set up so that for every day that the employee uses only nine boxes, he gets 50¢. If he reaches this goal every day of a five day work week, he gets $2.50. If he were able to keep this up for a month, he would receive $10. A certificate, a movie ticket, or something along those lines could also be awarded to him at the end of the month.

The truth is that the savings might be quite a bit larger than the worker's incentive. Let us say that the average cost for a company's metal scrap is about $200 per day for 300 pounds of metal. An incentive could be set up so that if these 300 pounds were reduced to 250 pounds per day, the employee would receive $2. At the end of the week, this would be $10 for the employee, and at the end of the month, $40. At the same time, reducing 300 hundred pounds of metal to 250 pounds of metal is saving the company $34 per day. So in this same month, the company would have saved $680 and paid out just $40 in incentives. If we add the $80 from the reduced wipe usage, the savings that the company would reap from just these two departments would be $760 per month. Minus the two incentive payouts, which combine to $50, the company' savings are $610 per month. This is $7,320 a year toward the goal of the $ 70,000 set out at the beginning. We can see, then, that incentives tied more closely to a person's day-to-day activity will result in a small outlay for the company but produce large dividends by the end of the year.

Another problem concerning an incentive too far removed from the worker's day-to-day activity, involves the principle that no incentive dollars will be paid out unless the company reaches a certain goal at the global level. So, for example, a company could set up a plan where the employees would each receive a monetary payout if they met an on-time delivery goal of 95 percent for three consecutive months, but in order to receive this, the company as a whole must meet a profit margin of five percent. The employees work very hard and achieve their goal. But the company does not meet it's goal at the global level, and the employees feel that all their efforts were in vain.

After this initial disappointment, they set about to work hard for the next three months with the hope of the company doing better in it's margin. If the company again fails to reach its margin, the employees receive no reward. Their efforts and enthusiasm begin to fade, and there comes a point when they give up on this extra push and return to their workaday pace. The employees feel they have no control over the company's goal, even though it controls whether the employees' incentives get paid out. The reason this incentive fails to work effectively is that the global goal is too far removed from the employees' contributing efforts. To make this incentive work, the employees must still be paid for their more immediate goal of a 95 percent on-time delivery. Thus their strong efforts will continue.

We can see an example of how this kind of incentive works effectively in the military's merit system. If a company of soldiers goes into a battle and loses, individual soldiers still receive rewards of individual merit for gallantry or bravery. Their individual efforts are recognized as beyond the ordinary, and they are given individual recognition to ensure that they continue at optimal performance. A greater number of awards are given if the battle is won. Individual recognition is not tied directly to the whole company, and the reward is near enough to a soldier's personal performance that it doesn't lose its effectiveness as a motivator.

Chapter Fourteen

Worker Competition

A huge opportunity to increase productivity and worker satisfaction is missed when competition is left out of the equation of incentives. Competition means completing a certain activity before another employee completes that same or similar activity. These activities could be accomplished during the same time period, as when running a race to the finish line, or the activity could be measured against a time clock where competitors are judged on the time it takes to complete the activity. It does not matter whether it's the same activity done in a shorter time or more activity done in the same time. All that matters is who gets more done measured against some standard.

A sports example will help. Two basketball teams do the same activities (e.g., shoot, jump, defend) in the same time frame as each other. But the winner is the team which racks up the most points in that set amount of time. On the other hand, while running a race, each athlete does the same activity but the goal is to do it in the shortest possible time.

Competition helps to create a beginning, middle, and end to an activity that otherwise lacks them. This is because in order to compete, clear boundaries are set so that some kind of judgment can be made as to whose efforts bring about the desired effect quicker or better. If there were no clear end, then there could be no clear winner. The end, therefore, leads to a definite beginning, and, from there, a middle. Anytime competition could be included in the work experience, it should be, as it helps employees fall into a mode where a beginning, middle, and end are apparent.

Competition is part of our very nature. Whenever there is an activity, it seems there is competition. When horses were the means of travel, we raced them. We still do. As soon as cars became the method of travel, we raced them. When it came to pulling, we set about to see who could pull the most. In lifting, we see who can lift the most. It seems if we do anything at all, we compete in it. We like competition so much that we devote hours of time to either watching sports or participating in them, and sports are simply activities that were made up so we could have a reason to compete.

Competition adds a certain pleasure to an activity. It tends to focus a person's attention in such ways as to make him operate more smoothly and perform the activity better. Also, the person seems to forget the hard work involved in the task. An example may be drawn from my own experience when a number of my friends and

I would stand around on a volleyball court and just hit a volleyball back and forth over the net. The ball seemed to always be hitting the ground as there was only a lackadaisical attitude and we only halfheartedly struck at the ball. Hence, there were no spectacular moves. However, once we formed teams and began to compete, a certain intensity developed and everyone played at a much higher level. For most, the quality of their playing made the activity much more pleasurable. A manager can exploit this competitive spirit, which is natural to all people, as an effective motivator.

Any time there are two shifts in which two groups of people are doing the same activity, there could be competition between them to see who can accomplish the most work in the same amount of time. Certain parameters, such as quality and safety, would remain fully in place. Within those parameters, competitive success should be rewarded. Whoever reaches a goal first or has reached the highest goals should be recognized. Inevitably, this brings out the best in both sets of workers. It gives them more pleasure on account of the thrill of competition and the hope of victory. It also increases efficiency because the more efficient workers would have the greater chance of reaching their goals first. There should be an incentive or reward to the person or team who wins, to take advantage of the competitive spirit.

Now, having extolled the virtues of competition it

must be noted that this incentive can also have deleterious effects and should be used with discretion. In the first place, people have different personalities and vary greatly in temperament. Where some thrive on competition, others find it quite intimidating and respond with anxiety. Losing can also be very distressing to some and can actually dampen their spirits—the opposite of what the manager is trying to accomplish. Finally, competition can easily turn friendships into adversarial relationships. In short, competition can be a valuable tool, but can also be fraught with unintended consequences.

Chapter Fifteen

Goals and Ends Are Not the Same

THOSE who have been managers and those who have had a great task to accomplish know the importance of goals. No successful enterprise has accomplished its purposes without a set of goals. Hence, every book written on how to be successful stresses the importance of clearly defined goals.

With this thought in mind, one may wonder why we placed stress on the importance of having a visible end to a job, even though this already seems to have been done by giving employees goals to reach. Most companies have interactive evaluations of their employees that give the employee goals that he is expected to reach to get merit pay increases or promotions. Even if this situation is not universal, most companies have an incentive program that ties rewards to the achievement of certain goals.

It would be true to say that goals are a kind of end. They are what most people strive for when they complete a certain activity, but goals differ from the kind of end to a task that I am emphasizing. Goals often are separate from the end of the particular art that a worker employs. To reach the goal of making a thousand dollars, one could employ many different arts. For example, one could write a piece of music and sell it. The end of the art of composing is when the last note of the piece is written. The goal of writing the piece might be the thousand dollars. The end of the art for the sculptor is the finished statue, not the money he sells it for. Incentives that are tied to goals were discussed in chapter ten. These are very useful in their own right but do not remove the drudgery that plagues the assembly line. These jobs lack the kind of end or finality that the composer or the sculptor enjoys. It is this kind of end that must be introduced back into the job experience if we are to return satisfaction to the workplace. This is what I mean by introducing visible and definable ends into the process. This is accomplished either by introducing visible boundaries into the process, like our boxes example, or by having a virtual reality brought about, such as a house being built.

Chapter Sixteen

Solutions to Rework and Rhythm Problems

THE first solution we will discuss addresses the problem of reworking. In our discussion on reworking, we already hit upon a way of making it less onerous. The experience of being disgusted, disappointed, or flat-out angry when we make a mistake occurs not only because we have ruined something that was intended to look beautiful or useful but also because the mistake has interrupted the natural flow of our art. Whenever this happens, the natural flow of emotions that accompanies the artist's work is also interrupted. These arrested emotions cause us pain. When one ruins an object he has been fashioning, all the work that went into the piece is wasted. The worker resents not being able to feel the joy of the completed art along with the wasted time and money.

We need to recognize that it is not the lost time or money that brings about the eruption of emotion but the interruption of the natural flow and end to which the artist was directed. By understanding this, a supervisor can better understand the resistance of his workers when work must be done over. To alleviate this problem, it is best if one person is responsible for reworking another's imperfect parts. The worker who repairs someone else's part does not have the emotional attachment that the first worker had. He can approach the defective piece as a new project and set about fixing it with a beginning, middle, and end to his work. As long as the worker understands that he is a problem solver and fixer of imperfect parts, then he approaches each project as that kind of craftsman and will set up his workstation for each piece to have a beginning, middle, and end. His satisfaction lies in the fixing of defective pieces.

We have seen how essential it is for a worker to be able to work in the natural mode of the craftsman. We saw the tremendous disruption that breaking the craftsman's rhythm creates. It should be clear now that anything a supervisor can do to aid in blocking unwanted distractions that assail the worker will aid in maximizing the worker's productivity. The incentives we have discussed can be applied to different parts of the worker's activities and can greatly augment his activity, but to interrupt his natural flow is very costly.

For example, if an employee has a responsibility that requires receiving phone calls, the supervisor should have certain times set aside when this worker can devote time to those issues. Again we can see that the lost productivity of this worker is far too costly not to address. Setting aside time for the worker to take care of business outside the natural flow of his work will make for a much more contented employee, and the company will avoid huge losses by preventing unnecessary drains on his productivity.

Chapter Seventeen

A Brighter Future

THE study of the craftsman holds within it the key to a brighter future for our next generation of workers who labor for the goods of man. Not only will it inspire those who have the desire and the means to strike out on their own and ply their trade as independent craftsman once more, it will also provide an impetus to many who labor in factories to install measures that will enhance their enjoyment of work. Those whose task it is to manage the work of others will be armed with a fuller understanding of the nature of man as an artist, and they can improve the workplace for his benefit.

Let us, then, briefly review the main points raised in this work, so that armed with a new spirit of hope and understanding, we can go forth refreshed and eager to do our part for the common good.

When we looked very closely into the activities of the craftsman as he set about his work, we found a definable beginning, middle and end to his activity; and this enabled us to discover the emotions that accompanied each stage of the work. We saw that there were times when the work could become tedious, and tiredness and depression ensue. The craftsman had the advantage of being rescued from this state by an approaching end to his task, by the coming about of a finished, visible end to his labors. The emotional joy he felt at this completion rescued him from the negative emotions one could fall into when work becomes monotonous, a common problem for the modern factory worker.

We found that the condition of the artisan changed dramatically with the introduction of concepts that took on a defined methodology with the publication of Adam Smith's The Wealth of Nations, which extolled the virtues of the division of labor and specialization. These concepts were seized upon with great excitement by those who had capital to invest as machines made mass production possible. Drives for efficiency and increased production made the possibility of great wealth a heady goal for some, and they capitalized on these new concepts—the same concepts that drive our industry today. Unfortunately, we suffer from most of the same maladies that afflicted them at the time of the Industrial Revolution. The particular malady we are addressing here is the widespread dissatisfaction of our workingmen with their jobs.

We discovered the roots of this dissatisfaction in the introduction of the division of labor and specialization, which obscured the beginning, middle, and end of most jobs for most workers. When these notions became obscure, work became a continuous stream, resulting in monotony, drudgery, and a slave–like mentality. We noted that the modern worker is stuck in the emotional state of a craftsman stuck between points of definition—a state of drudgery that we all wish to escape as quickly as possible.

It has become obvious now that this is a very unnatural state for man to be in. Perpetual work is not a natural activity for man because we are all artists or craftsmen by nature and it is natural that our labors result in an end.

Human beings set about every activity with a course of activity to follow according to a definite beginning, middle, and end and unless this is realized no real progress can be made in a laborer's condition.

We saw in our discussions concerning the emotions aroused in a craftsman under natural conditions that unnatural conditions produce boredom, frustration, anger and despondency. Consequently, we can conclude that many of the advantages of Adam Smith's model for increased productivity are canceled out by these negative emotions. As job satisfaction wanes, productivity does as well.

Moreover, worker dissatisfaction has even more serious social consequences than just the material loss of anticipated wealth, as it even infects man's life when his workday is done. Suffice it to say that at this point a remedy such as we have outlined in this work is sorely needed.

We have looked at traditional incentive programs and

found them wanting. Although they can work as motivators, and do inspire some workers to greater effort in expectation of greater reward, they ultimately fail to address the syndrome in the work itself that results in the depressed moods of the workplace. A true solution depends on restoring the craftsman model to the workplace. Only then will traditional incentive programs be effective. These traditional incentive programs will only reach their full motivational potential when the worker experiences the emotions of the craftsman through the whole process of his work. Thereby he will have the joy that follows completion and supervisors will recognize that reward and recognition should be given when that joy is being felt.

We suggested many ways to introduce the experience of the craftsman into the work place. Any time an employer identifies a work experience in his factory that is akin to the experience of the craftsman he should emphasize the beginning, middle, and end of the work and tie his incentives to that. We saw the necessity of establishing artificial boundaries where none can be found, to relieve the deadening effect of monotony. One of the most exciting possibilities in this regard lies in the realm of virtual reality.

With all these suggestions in hand, and as the concepts of this book are absorbed and the minds of others applied to them, a better work environment can be created. Through patient investigation, we have discovered the reasons why so many workers are unhappy in their jobs, in the midst of a material abundance made possible by division of labor and specialization. Now that we have identified the reasons for this condition, we can confidently pursue, achieve and provide solutions to this serious social problem.

www.ingramcontent.com/pod-product-compliance
Lightning Source LLC
Chambersburg PA
CBHW071409290426
44108CB00014B/1748